Contents

- **2** Introduction/The Romans
- **4** Cirencester 30 CE
- **6** Cirencester 65 CE
- **8** Cirencester 200 CE
- **10** The Amphitheatre
- **12** The Roman Town Wall
- **14** The Hare Mosaic
- **16** The Seasons Mosaic
- **18** The Hunting Dogs Mosaic
- **20** The Orpheus Mosaic
- **22** The Venus Mosaic
- **24** The Hypocaust
- **26** The Basilica and Forum
- **28** The Macellum *(Market)*
- **30** The Roman Theatre
- **32** The Roman Army
- **34** Roman Cirencester today

Symbols used in this guide

Outlines of Roman walls
(still visible)

Outlines of Roman walls
(no longer visible)

Amphitheatre
Roman points of interest
(still visible)

Basilica
Roman points of interest
(no longer visible)

 Corinium Museum
Displaying multiple artefacts including:
Hare Mosaic (P 14)
Seasons Mosaic (P 16)
Hunting Dogs Mosaic (P 18)
Orpheus Mosaic (P 20)
The Venus Mosaic (P 22)
Hypocaust (P 24)
The Roman Army (P32)

Cirencester looking north, 200 CE.

Introduction

Cirencester is a beautiful Gloucestershire town located in the famous Cotswolds. Before the Roman invasion the town was unoccupied land which was part of the territory of the *Dobunni* tribe. After the invasion the site was a strategic intersection of Roman roads, which developed into Britain's second largest Roman town called *Corinium Dobunnorum*. Later, over the centuries the town became known as Cirencester.

This guide explores the period from 30 CE to 370 CE. After this date the Roman Empire started a gradual decline and by 410 CE Britain was under constant attack by marauding Anglo-Saxons.

The guide brings to life how Roman Corinium could have looked, with full-colour images all looking north and detailed maps showing where each site is in present-day Cirencester.

Towns and cities
The Romans defined towns and cities differently to how we do in the present day. They had three main types of town:
• *A Colonia, which was a rough equivalent of a city.*
• *A Municipium, which was slightly less important than a colonia.*
• *A Civitas capital, which was a broad equivalent of a large market town.*
The Romans called Pre-Roman towns 'oppida'.

The Romans

The city of Rome in central Italy was formed around 800 BCE and grew over the centuries into the Roman Empire, which covered most of Europe and northern Africa. It was a highly sophisticated and technologically advanced society, with a huge army, major roads and large cities.

Britain at that time was a mysterious place with fierce tribes and valuable metals, which became the focus of an attempted invasion in 55 BCE and 54 BCE by Julius Caesar.

Those invasions were repelled by local tribes and the Romans did not try again to invade Britain for almost 100 years.

By 43 CE the Emperor Claudius *(who needed the army's support)* decided to invade Britain, which was weakened by the death of King Cunobelin of the Trinovantes, who lived in Camulodunum *(Colchester)*. Gathering his forces, Claudius set his sights on Colchester, later moving across the country including the area which is now Cirencester...

Visiting Cirencester

Cirencester lies about 90 miles west of London.

The Corinium Museum in the town centre has excellent exhibits showing what life was like in Roman Cirencester, including a collection of some of the best Roman mosaics in the country. Outside the museum, you can also see the remains of the amphitheatre on the edge of the town and a small section of the Roman Wall.

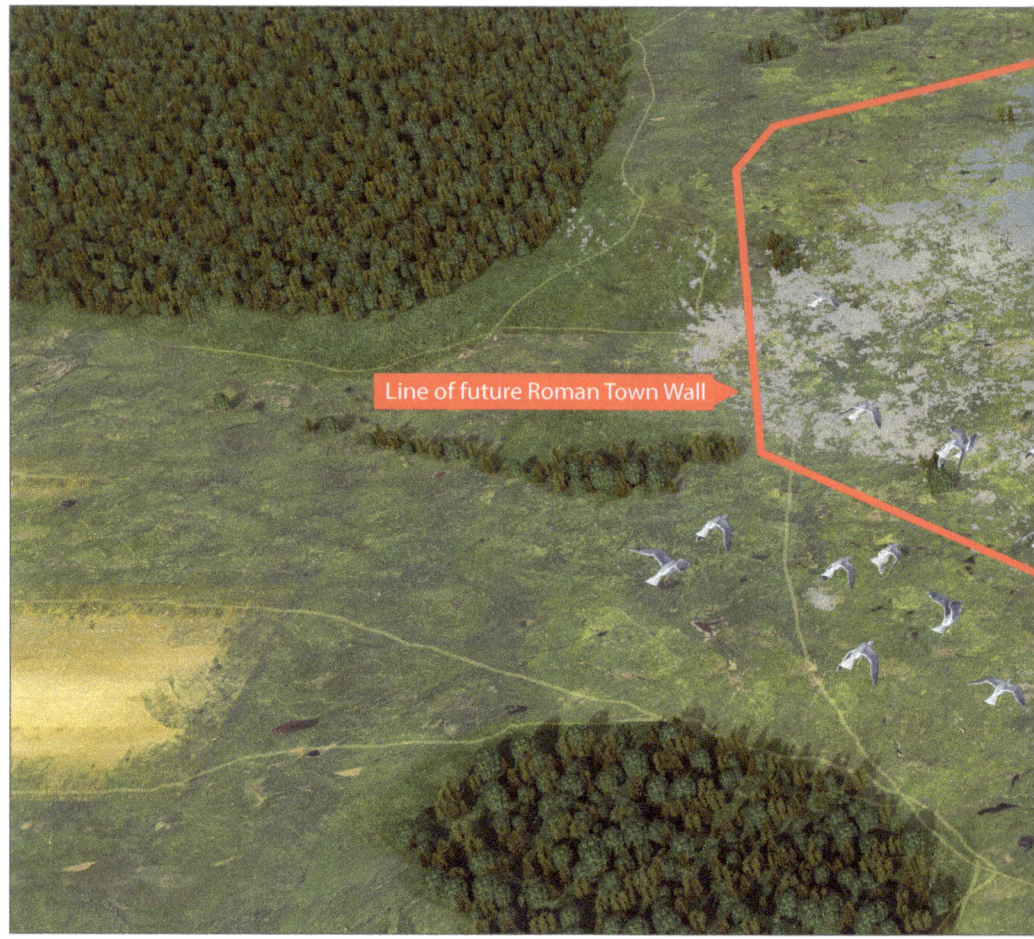

Cirencester, looking north, 30 CE.

Cirencester 30 CE

Before the Romans invaded there was no settlement where Cirencester now stands. The future site of Cirencester was part of the lands of the *Dobunni* tribe with an *oppidum* located a short distance north, at Bagendon. An *oppidum* (loosely translated as 'town' in Latin) was a large fortified Iron Age settlement.

The Dobunni tribe had territory which roughly covered modern day Gloucestershire and parts of the surrounding counties. Unlike many other bordering tribes such as the *Silures (based around southern Wales)* the Dobunni were not warlike and readily accepted the Romans without conflict. The Romans established a fortress around 49 CE, south of the oppidum, at the junction of several important roads, although in a slightly marshy area.

Find out more

There are no visible remains of Pre-Roman Cirencester as it was mostly marshland. Partial remains of the oppidum can just be seen around Bagendon, 4 miles (6 km) to the north of Cirencester.

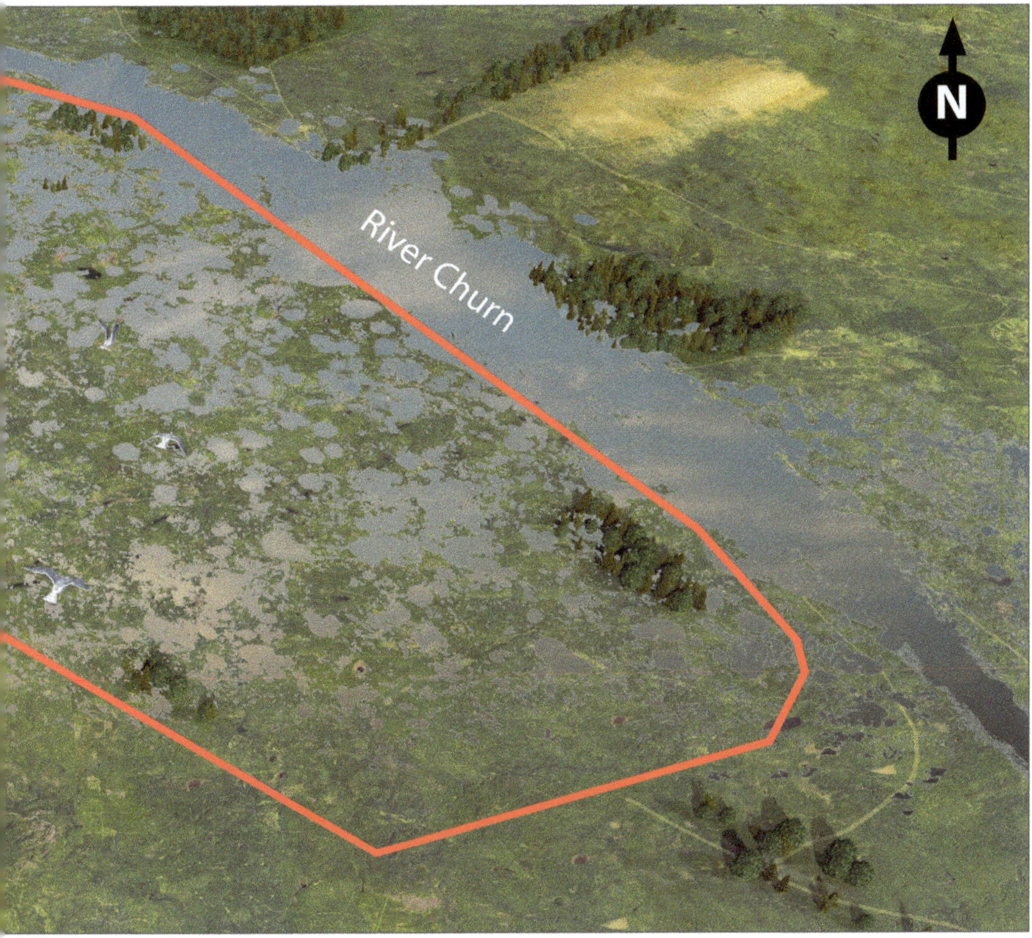

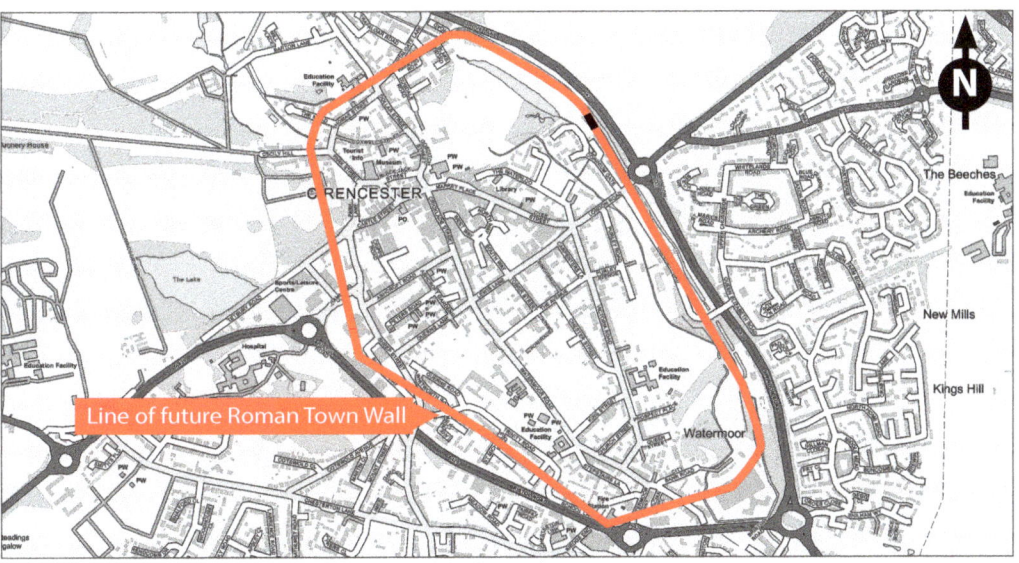

Line of future Roman Town Wall

Contains Ordnance Survey data © Crown copyright and database right 2023

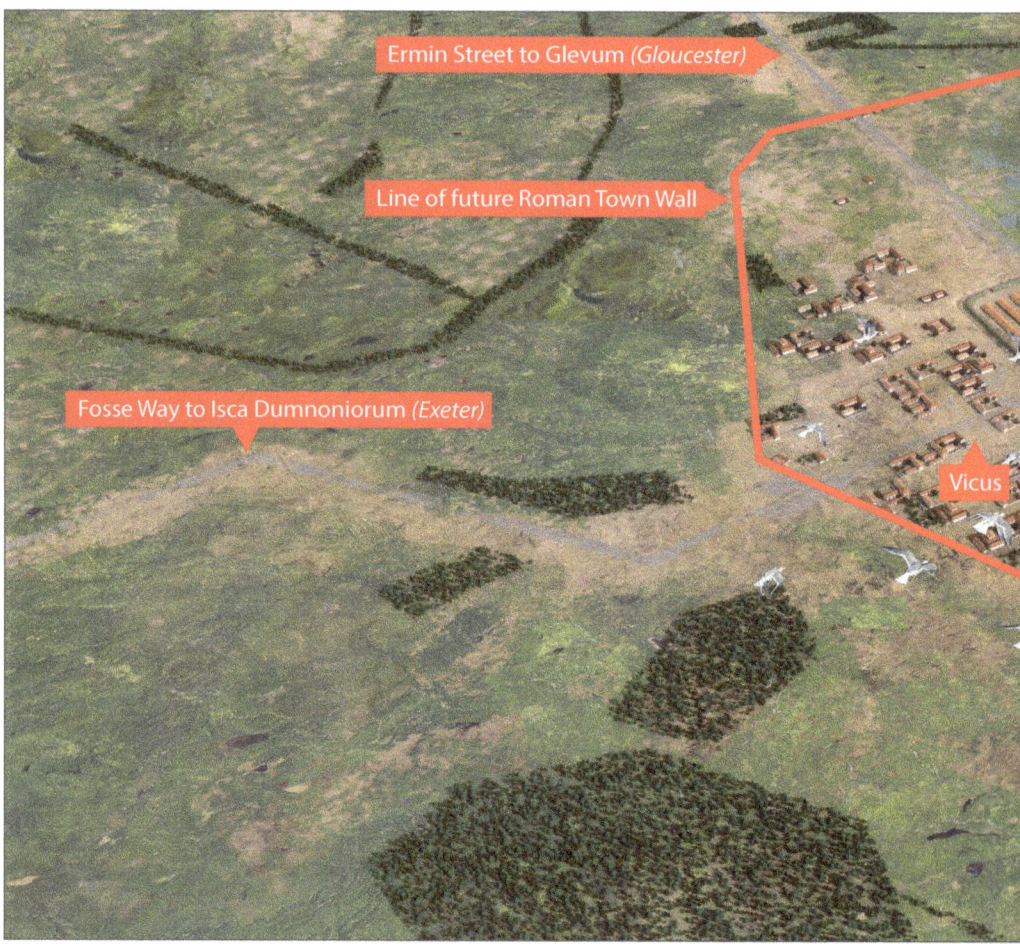

Cirencester, looking north, 65 CE. A speculative view of how the Roman Fortress may have looked.

Cirencester 65 CE

A fortress was placed at the strategic junction of roads built by the Romans. These roads were built to get troops to where they were needed as quickly as possible.

Roman roads were planned by specialised Roman *Mensors* (military surveyors) who could with great accuracy connect two locations via the shortest route. For example Ermin Street connects Exeter to Cirencester.

The historical records are slightly unclear but the fortress may have been manned by an auxiliary cavalry unit, possibly part of the *Legio II Augusta (Second Legion 'Augustus')* which was moving around the south west of Britain.

By 75 CE the garrison at the fortress was transferred to other areas in Britain. The fortress had been dismantled and by 80 CE the *Vicus (equivalent to a village)* that bordered the fortress became the town called *Corinium Dobunnorum* (modern day Cirencester).

Find out more

There are no visible remains of the Roman fortress. Items used by the Roman Army can be seen in the Corinium Museum. The main image is a speculative interpretation of how the fortress might have looked and its possible size.

Fosse Way to Lindum *(Lincoln)*
N
Auxiliary fortress
Ermin Street to Calleva Atrebatum *(Near Silchester)*

N
Line of future Roman Town Wall
The Beeches
New Mills
Kings Hill
Watermoor
Archery House
The Lake

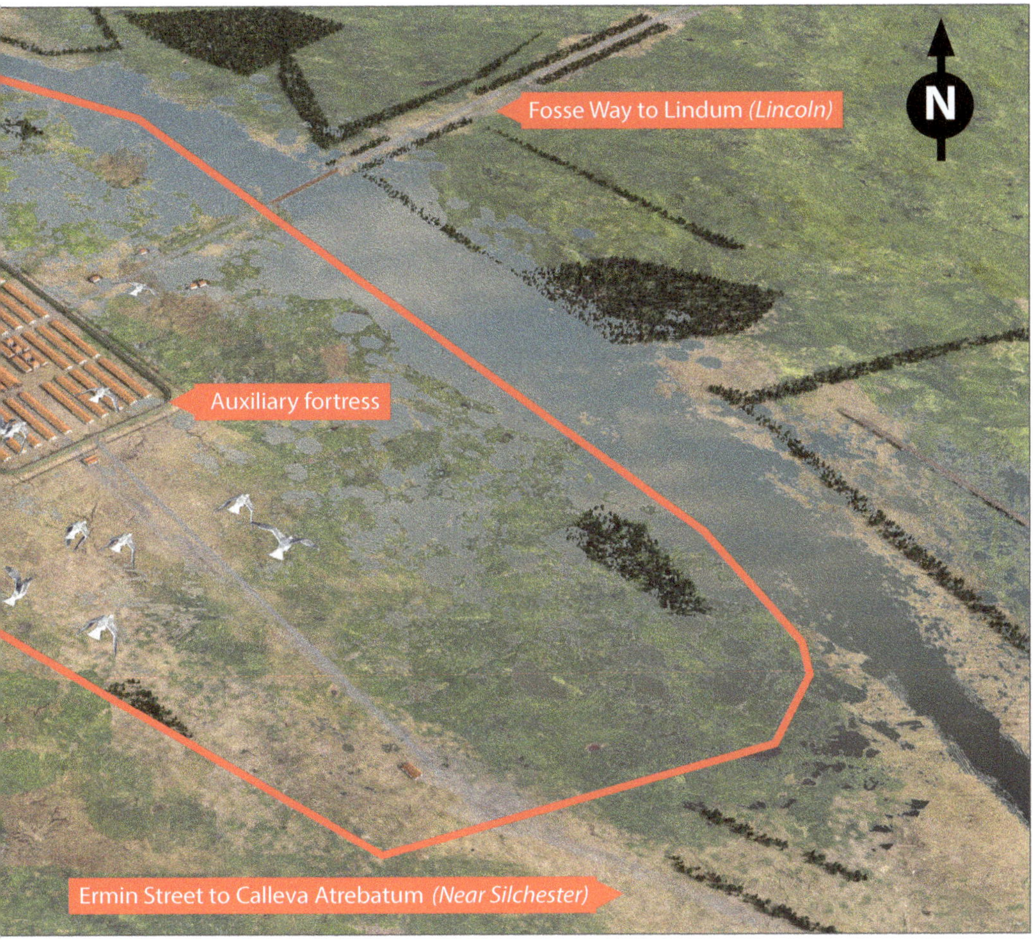

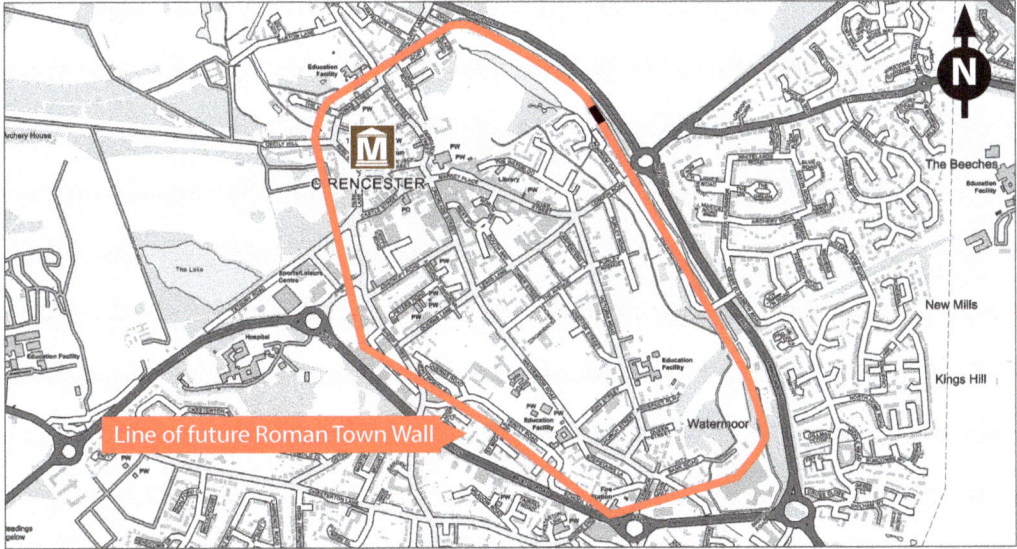

Cirencester, looking north, 200 CE.

Cirencester 200 CE

Corinium Dobunnorum (Cirencester) grew into Britain's second largest Roman town. Basic earth defences were improved over time with a stone town wall. In later centuries, significant amounts of military equipment were produced here. The main image shows a speculative view of how Cirencester could have looked. While some buildings such as the Forum, Basilica and the Town Wall have been found, other such as public baths, temples and granaries have not yet been found, but a town of this size is likely to have had them. The image above shows some possible locations of these sites. A large amphitheatre was also constructed to entertain the inhabitants. The town continued to thrive until the gradual collapse of the Roman Empire around 412 CE. After that time, it was largely abandoned but some areas were occupied by the Anglo-Saxons and later, the Normans.

Find out more
Most of Roman Cirencester is no longer visible except for the remains of the amphitheatre and a small section of the City Wall.
The Corinium Museum in the centre of Cirencester, has many Roman artefacts, including impressive large mosaics.

Town Wall
Town Wall
N

Town Wall
Town Wall
Amphitheatre
CIRENCESTER
The Beeches
New Mills
Kings Hill
Watermoor
N

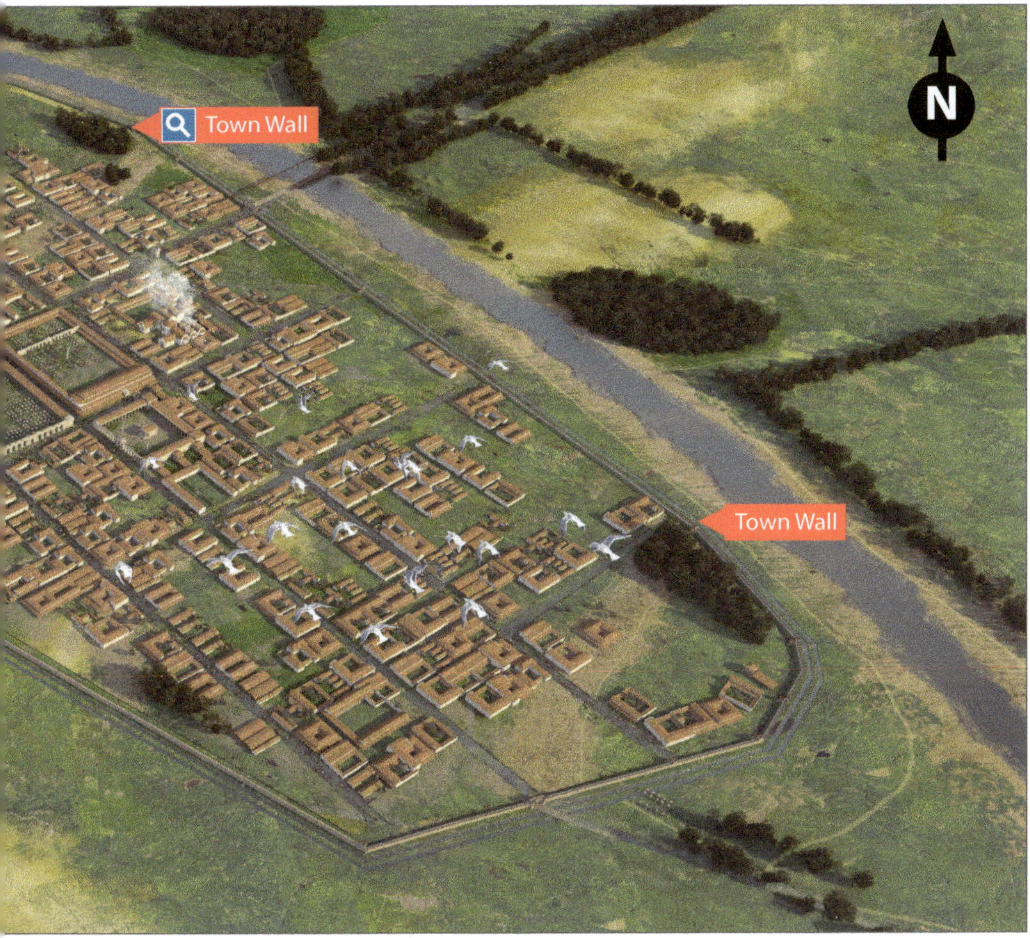

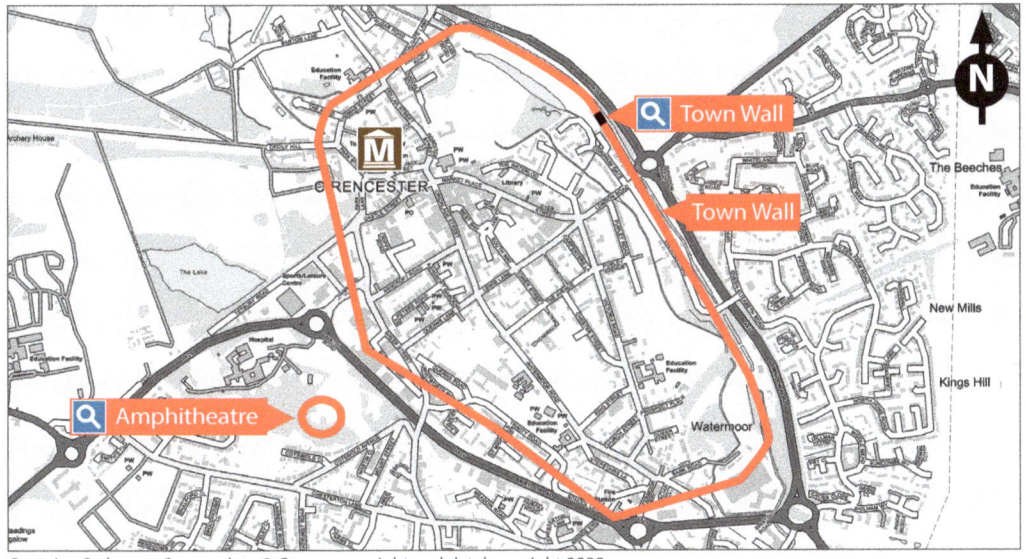

Site of the Amphitheatre, looking north, 200 CE.

The Amphitheatre

In the 2nd century the oval amphitheatre was built to provide entertainment for the inhabitants of Corinium. The base of the amphitheatre *(still visible)* was made from stone and topped by a wooden structure.
It would have been a huge building seating around 8000 people, all wanting a view of the gladiators fighting.
Shops and stalls would have been clustered around the base of the amphitheatre, selling food to the crowds.
Contests usually began with the gladiators *(Latin for swordsmen)* paraded in front of the crowd, with music playing. These contests often started in the morning, with the victors celebrated in the middle of the day.
Bears, wolves, criminals and Christians were all forced to fight in the *'games'* held inside the amphitheatre.

Find out more
Although most of the amphitheatre is no longer visible, huge sections of its base can be seen just south of the present day town centre as marked by the red circle on the map.

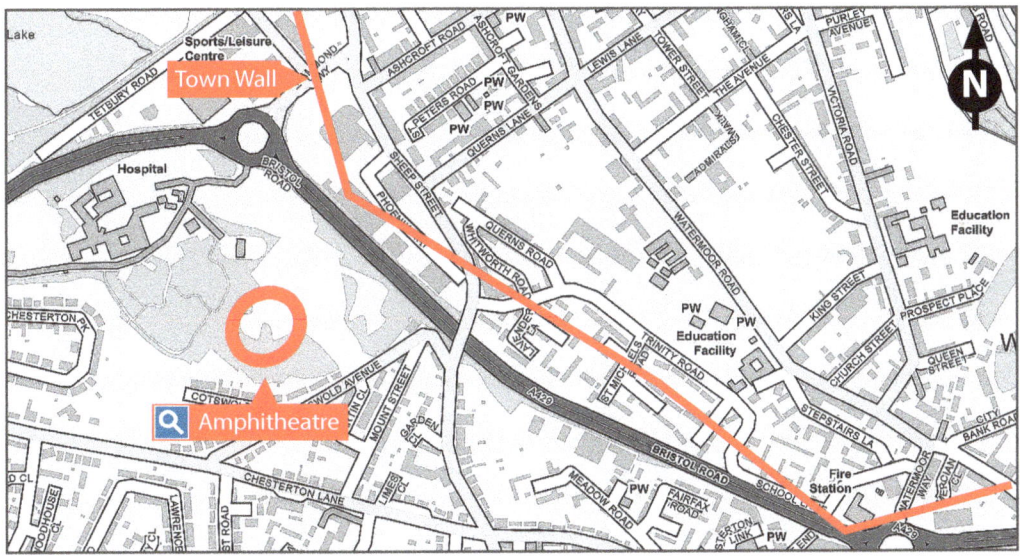

The Roman Town Wall, looking north, 200 CE.

Close-up view of the Bath Gate in 200 CE

The Roman Town Wall

Around 140 CE construction was completed on the Town Wall, which was probably made of wood. By the 3rd century the Town Wall had been rebuilt from stone. It was about 6 metres *(19.6 feet)* high and possibly 2.4 metres *(7.8 feet)* thick and 3.2 kilometres *(2 miles)* long. Around the wall there were at least four gatehouses and many towers guarded by centurions, legionaries and auxiliaries. The main image shows how the Town Wall was a continuous circuit, so that troops could move to any part rapidly. At the end of most streets or corners there were guard-towers which would be used as observation posts. Outside were defensive ditches for further protection, these were often 2 metres *(6 feet)* deep and v-shaped. Sometimes the ditches surrounding Roman towns were filled with water for extra security.

Find out more
Most of the Roman Town Wall was robbed for building material over the centuries. The only part still visible can be seen in the western section of the Abbey Grounds.

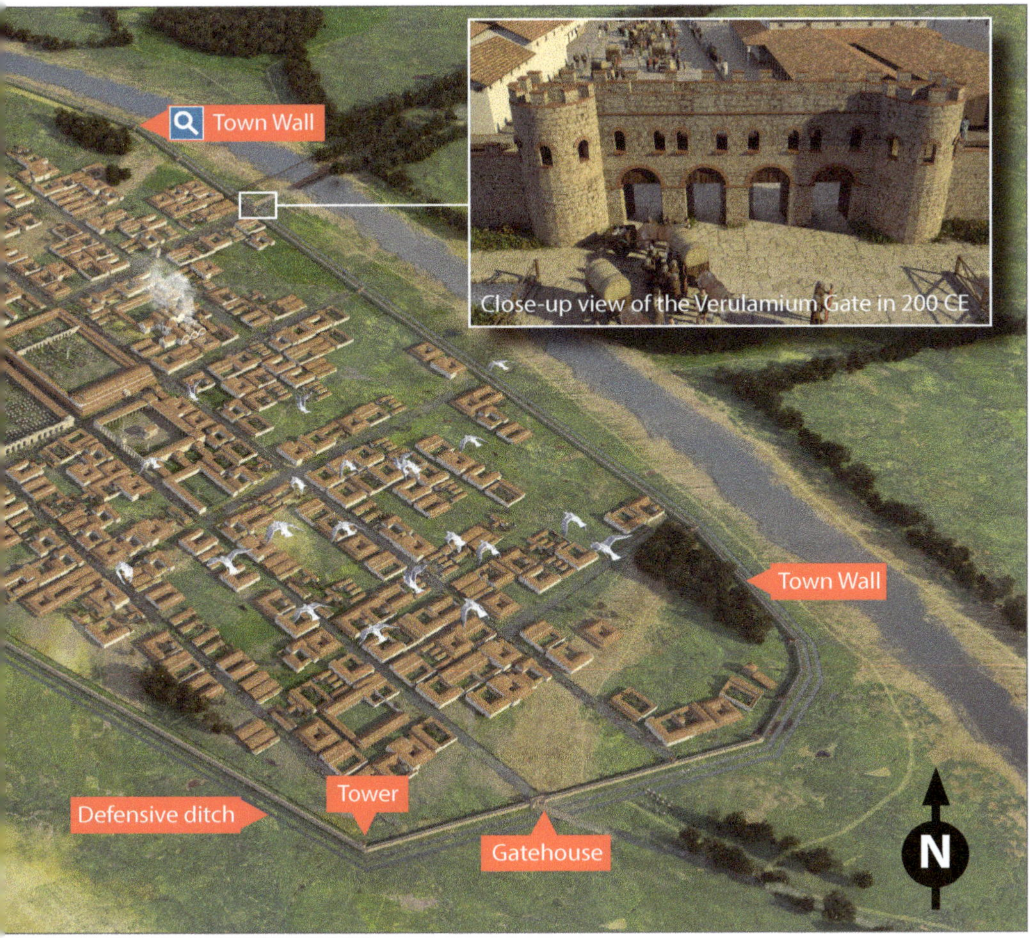
Town Wall
Close-up view of the Verulamium Gate in 200 CE
Town Wall
Tower
Defensive ditch
Gatehouse
N

Town Wall
Town Wall
N
CIRENCESTER
The Beeches
New Mills
Kings Hill
Watermoor

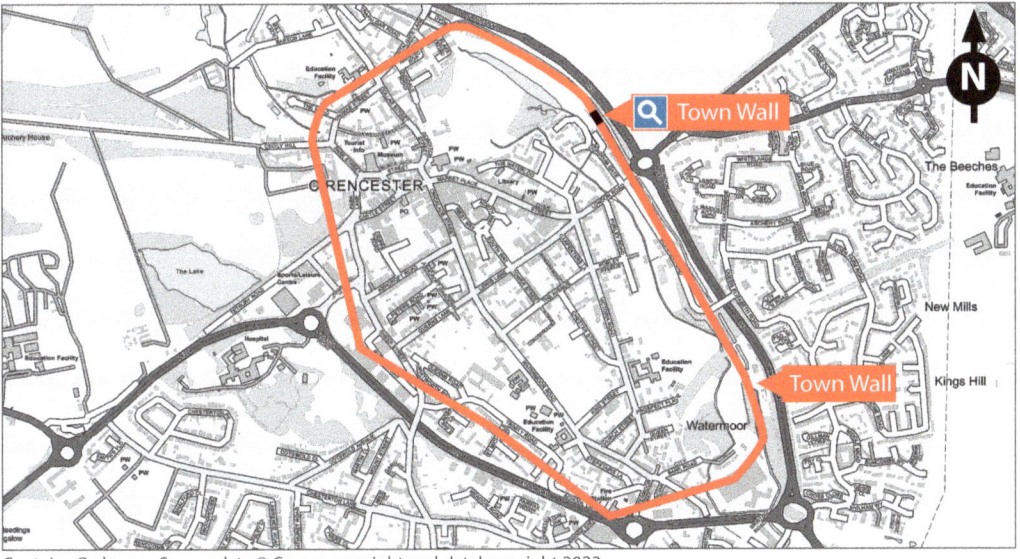

Possible interior of the building which housed the Hare Mosaic, around 310 CE.

The Hare Mosaic

Many of the wealthy houses in Roman Britain had elaborate mosaics on the floors. Mosaics are made up of hundreds of small squares of coloured tiles called *tesserae*.

These tesserae were laid into a flat surface covered with mortar, which made them long lasting and allowed for complex designs. One such design was found in Cirencester depicting a hare, which dates from around the 4th century. Of the few examples of mosaics found featuring hares, they are usually shown in hunting scenes, rather than feeding, as shown in this example. The mosaic was later covered over with a channelled hypocaust as part of a small bathhouse, which then protected it until it was rediscovered on Beeches Road *(see page 24)*. Archaeologists also discovered a circular mosaic which was located in the next room. The image above includes a speculative view of the circular mosaic, based on one found in Rome.

Find out more

The Hare Mosaic can be seen in the Corinium Museum. The mosaic was originally in a small room as shown in the image above, and was part of a large complex found on Beeches Road in the 1970s. The section with the birds and a two-handled jug was found as shown here, but is rotated $180°$ in the Corinium Museum to help people better appreciate the mosaic.

A view showing how much of the mosaic can be seen in the present day.

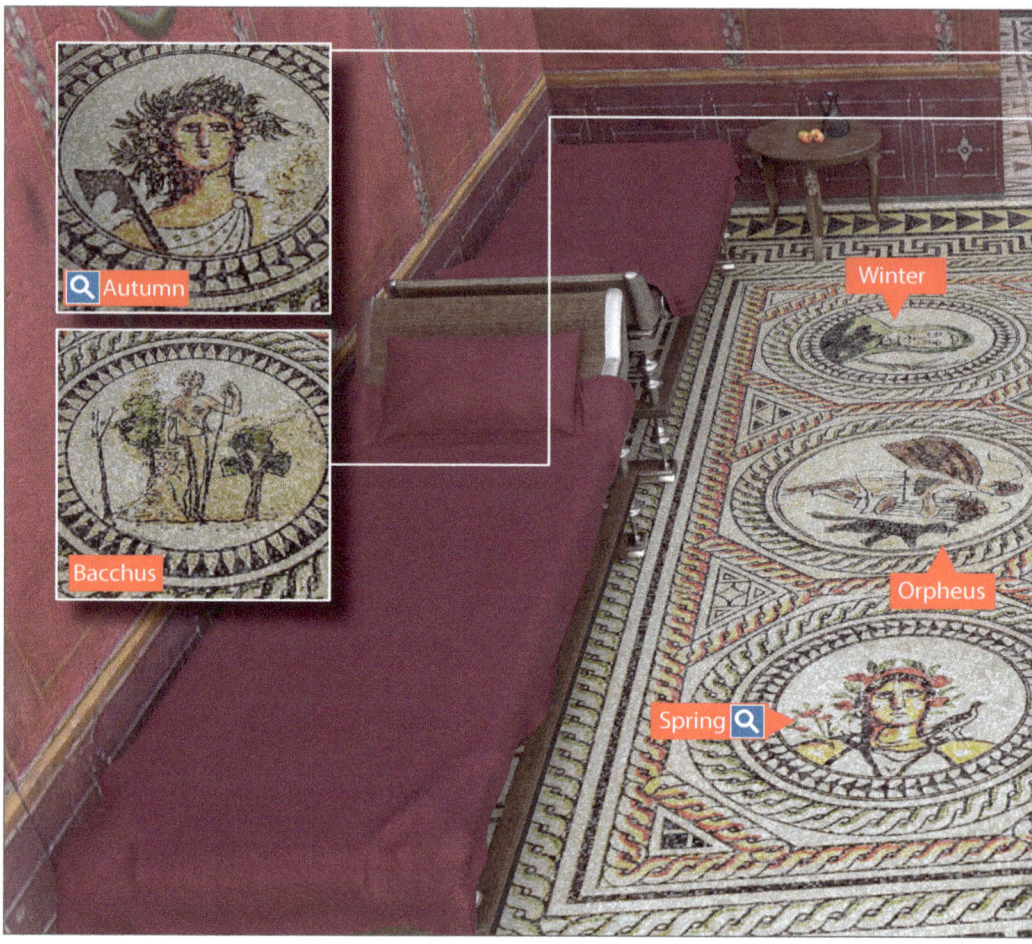

Possible interior of the townhouse which housed the Seasons Mosaic, around the 2nd century.

The Seasons Mosaic

The Seasons Mosaic was unearthed in 1849 in Dyer Street, Cirencester. The seasons were a common theme in many Roman mosaics, here we can see:

Spring- **Flora** Goddess of flowers.
Summer- **Ceres** Goddess of agriculture.
Autumn- **Pomona** Goddess of the orchard.
Winter- Possibly **Saturnus** God of sowing, who was celebrated around mid-winter (this image no longer survives).

Another common theme was characters from Roman mythology such as *Actaeon*. He was a character from classical mythology who angered *Diana (the goddess of the hunt)*. She slowly transformed him into a stag and then he was attacked by his own dogs, which is shown in the 2nd century mosaic. *Bacchus* the Roman god of wine and fertility is also shown, with his *preceptor (roughly translated as teacher) Silenus*, and a *bacchante (a priest or follower of Bacchus)*.

Find out more

The Seasons Mosaic can be seen in the Corinium Museum. Note that some of the details shown on the mosaic are speculative, as they no longer survive. For example the central image suggests a possible image of a Centaur, although some think it may have been the winged horse 'Pegasus'. The mosaic might have been placed in a house's Vestibulum (reception hall). The mosaic in the far room is speculative.

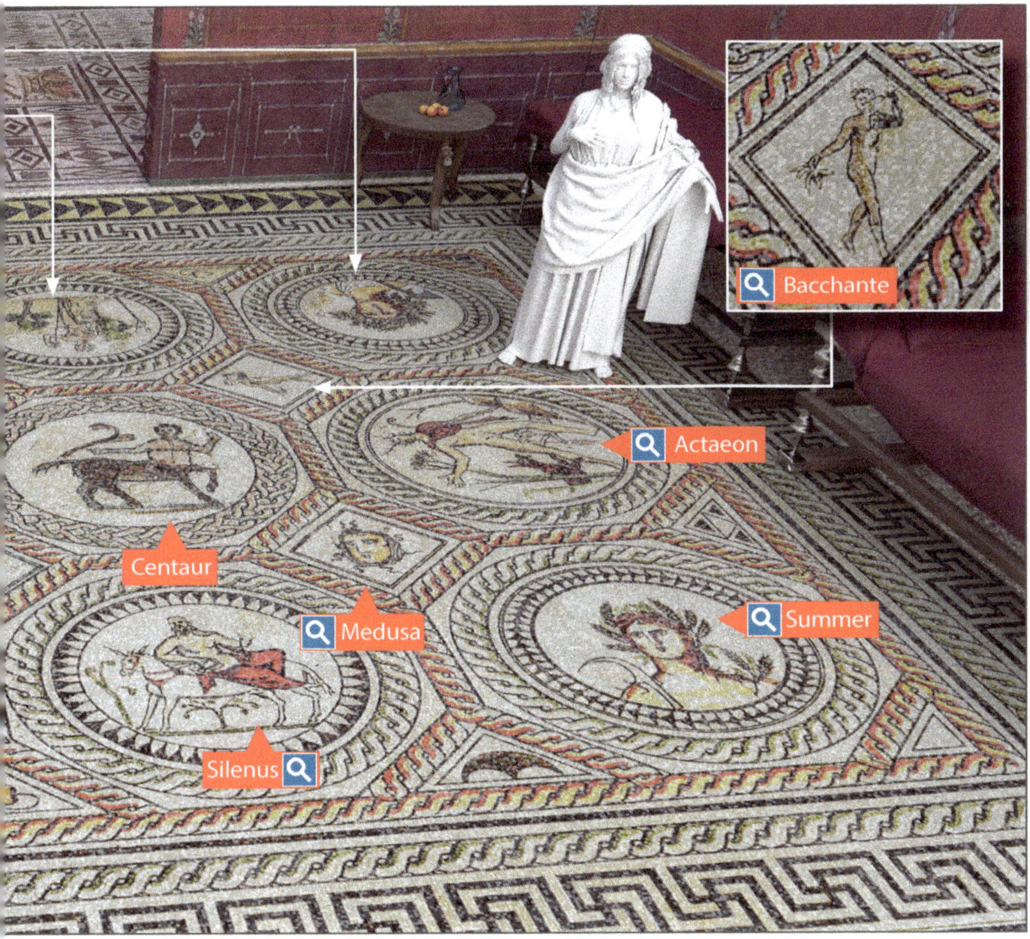

A view showing how much of the mosaic can be seen in the present day.

Possible interior of the townhouse which housed the Hunting Dogs Mosaic, around the 3rd century.

The Hunting Dogs Mosaic

The Hunting Dogs Mosaic was found in 1849 on Dyer Street in Cirencester. It seems that half of the mosaic was relaid in Roman times as it may have partially collapsed into a hypocaust *(Roman under-floor heating)*. When the mosaic was repaired, the design seems to have incorporated geometric patterns rather than the sea theme including sea creatures and *Oceanus/Neptune*[1]. Not a great deal of effort was made to match the original. It may have been originally part of a Roman townhouse and might have been located in a *Triclinium (dining room)*. Here the owner would have entertained guests, possibly wealthy merchants or politicians.

Find out more

The Hunting Dogs Mosaic can be seen in the Corinium Museum. Note that some of the details shown on the mosaic are speculative, as they no longer survive. For example the central image suggests hares being chased by dogs, which is based on a similar mosaic in Tunisia. Now only the dogs survive on the mosaic.

1. *Oceanus was a Greek god, often shown with crab claws on his head, while Neptune was the Roman god of freshwater and the sea.*

A view showing how much of the mosaic can be seen in the present day.

Possible interior of the building which housed the Orpheus Mosaic, around the 4th century.

The Orpheus Mosaic

This mosaic dates from the 4th century and depicts Orpheus surrounded by animals. The mosaic might have been placed in a house's *Vestibulum (reception hall)*. It was found in a house just outside Cirencester and might have belonged to a merchant or local dignitary. Orpheus was a legendary character from Greek mythology who was said to have travelled with *Jason and the Argonauts* to capture the *Golden Fleece*. He also travelled to the underworld to try to save his wife *Eurydice*. He was able to charm anything alive with his *lyre (a small harp)*. This is shown on the mosaic with the animals surrounding him such as the large cats, a rare mythological *Griffon (or Gryphon)* and birds. Mosaics such as this one acted as focal points in the homes of the wealthy. The Romans' use of Greek mythology shows how they adopted other civilisations' heritage and technology to improve their own civilisation.

Find out more

The Orpheus Mosaic can be seen in the Corinium Museum. The image above shows a possible room where the mosaic might have been located. Many Roman houses also had elaborate wall paintings to help make the rooms seem much larger. Note the fox to the right of Orpheus. The fox features in many Orpheus mosaics and is thought to have had a special connection with Orpheus. The mosaic in the far room is speculative.

A view showing how much of the mosaic can be seen in the present day.

Possible interior of the building which housed the Venus Mosaic, around the 4th century.

The Venus Mosaic

The Venus Mosaic was found in the 1970s at Kingscote (about 18 miles/29 km west of Cirencester) as part of a large archaeological dig. Most Roman mosaics used complex interweaving patterns, now known as *guilloche*, which were thought to represent infinity. Roman mosaics may have acted as conversation pieces with mythical figures on them, such as *Venus*[1] on this mosaic. Also shown on the mosaic is a *Cantharus vessel*[2]. The Romans would often build new mosaics or features over old mosaics. It is possible that they used mosaic pattern books to choose designs. Once a design was chosen it was then assembled on-site. The artist sometimes used flourishes such as red marks to tell others who had produced the mosaic.

1. Venus was the Roman goddess of love (originally the Greek goddess Aphrodite).
2. A Cantharus is a large two-handled drinking cup.

Find out more

The Venus Mosaic is marked as the **Kingscote mosaic** in the Corinium Museum. Also shown on the main image is the Lotus flower, another symbol of Venus, which represented regeneration. Note that some of the details on the mosaic are speculative, as they no longer survive. For example the image at the bottom right shows a sea griffon with dolphins, as seen in similar mosaics.

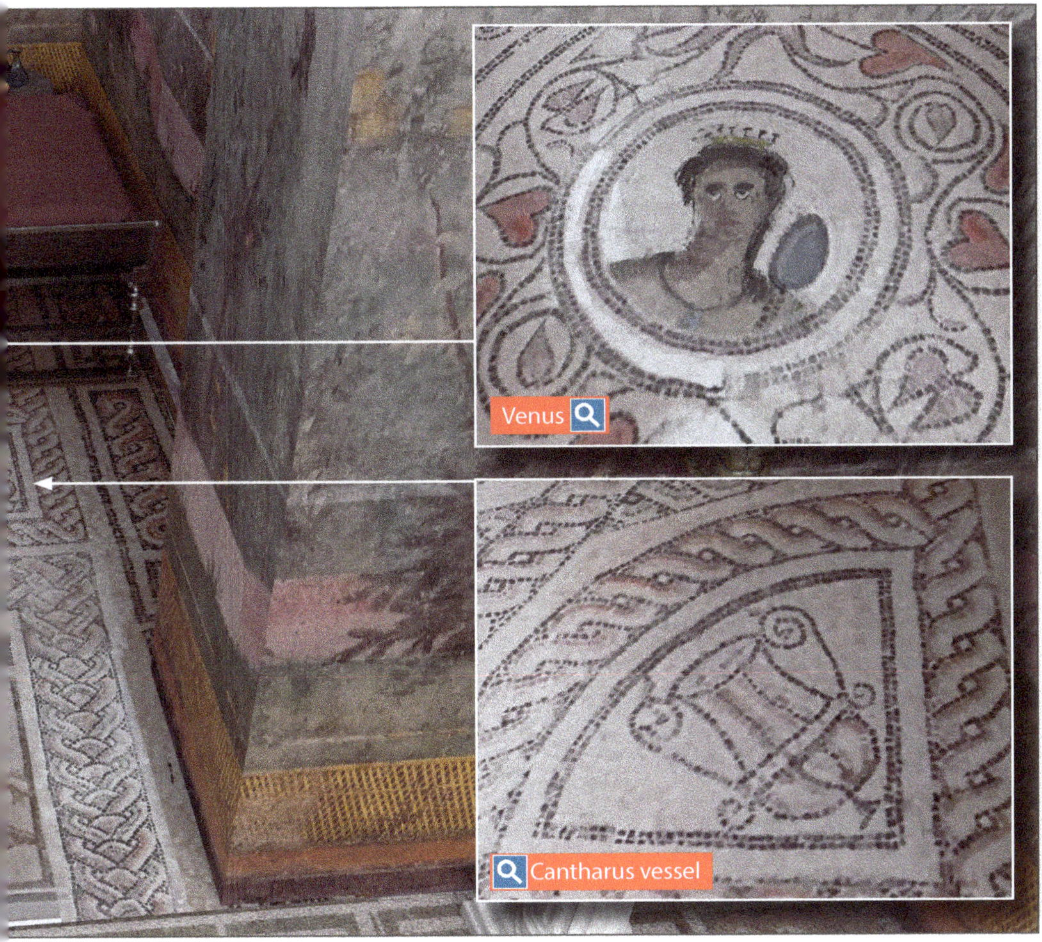

Venus

Cantharus vessel

A view showing how much of the mosaic can be seen in the present day.

How the Hypocaust could have looked around 370 CE.

The Hypocaust

The Romans were masters of innovation and construction. Many of their inventions were not replicated by others for hundreds of years. One example was heated floors which only in the last century became common again in domestic dwellings. The Romans had a system of heated floors which transferred heat from a furnace, usually run by slaves, under the floor. The floor was raised from the ground on small sets of columns or stacked bricks called pilae. The excess heat was vented through chimneys in the walls. This system was also used for public buildings such as baths. Less wealthy people would have had to heat their homes with open fires. The word *Hypocaust* came originally from the Greek words *Hypo (under)* and *caust (burnt)*. This hypocaust was actually built on top of the **Hare Mosaic** *(shown on page 14)* and a new mosaic was added, as well as a storeroom to house the furnace and wood.

Find out more
Part of a hypocaust can be seen inside the Corinium Museum, which has been laid out following a common arrangement seen in Roman buildings, using pilae (stacked brick pieces). The hypocaust shown above recreates the one found covering the Hare Mosaic. It used a slightly different method to direct the heat, called a channelled hypocaust. The red areas show parts removed to help understand the site.

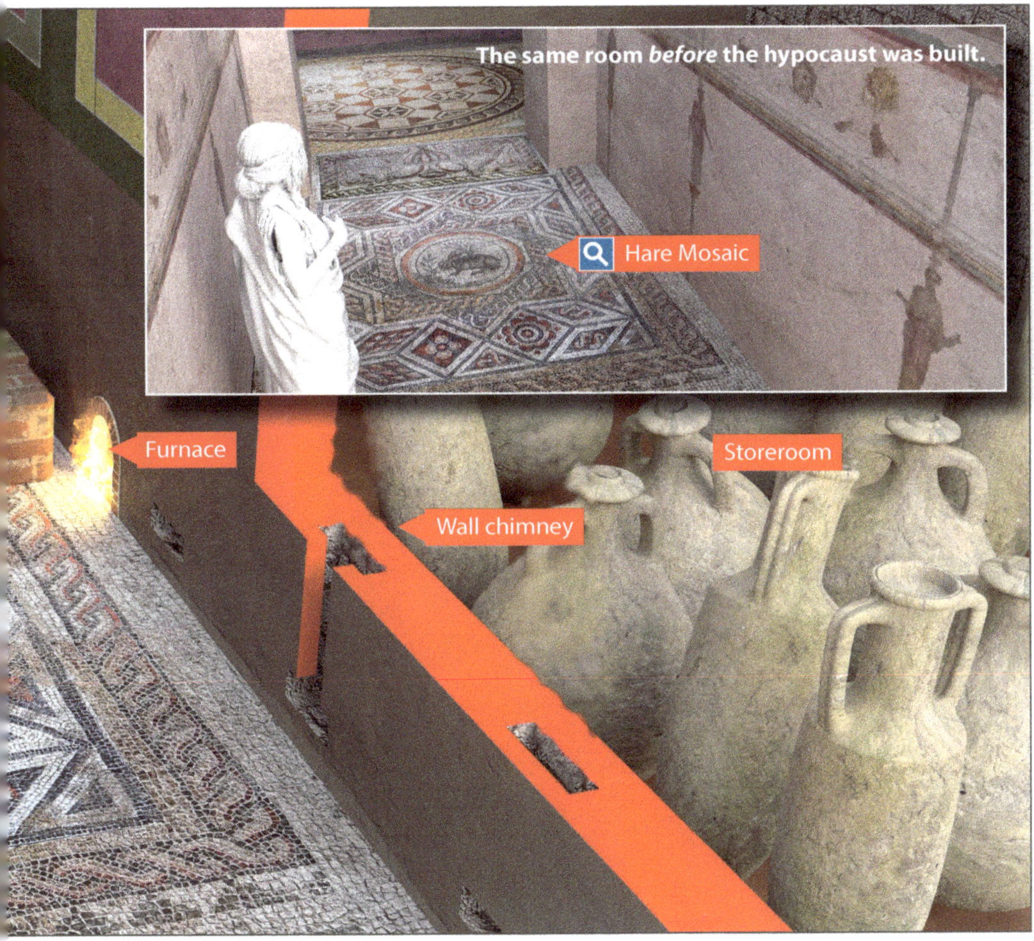

The same room *before* the hypocaust was built.

Hare Mosaic

Furnace

Wall chimney

Storeroom

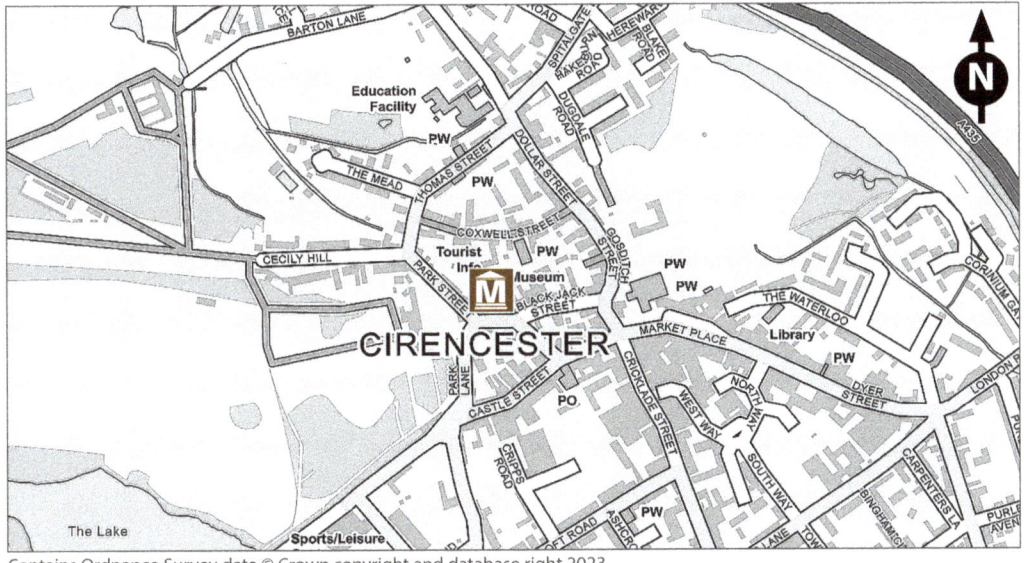

Contains Ordnance Survey data © Crown copyright and database right 2023

26. The Basilica and Forum

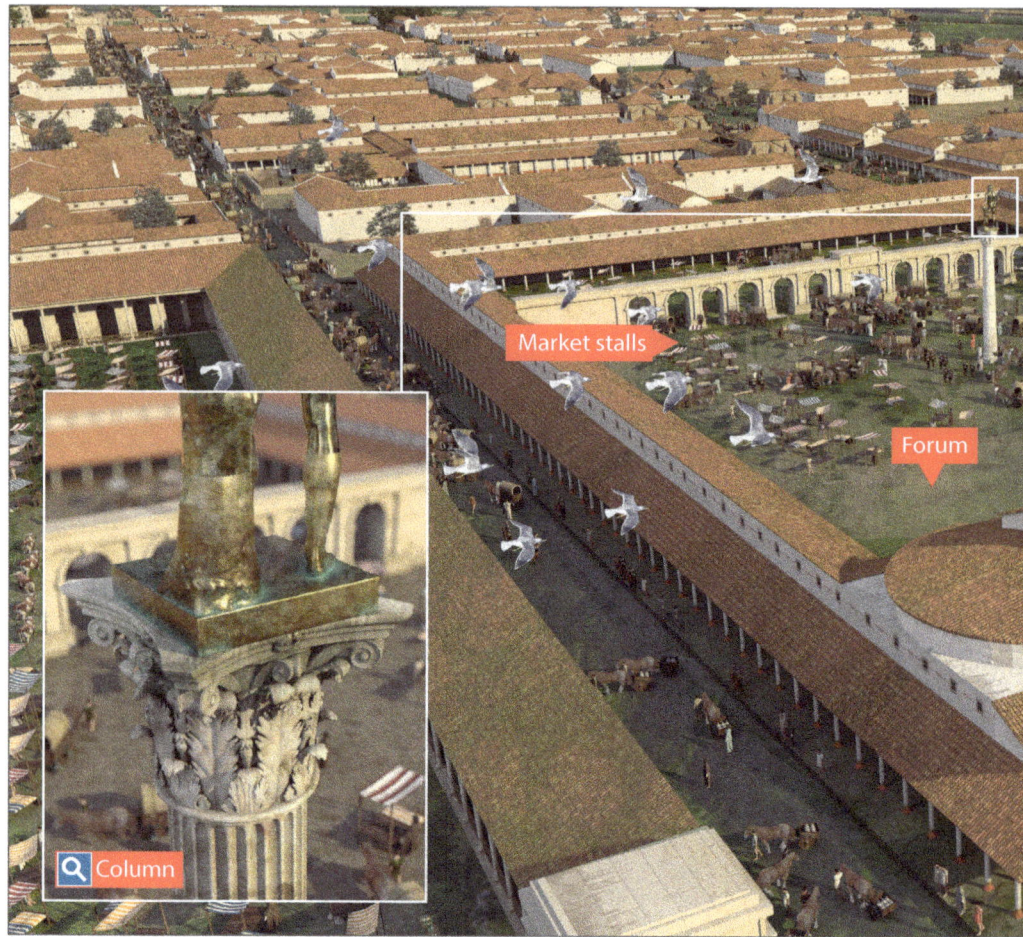

Site of the Basilica and Forum, looking north, 200 CE.

The Basilica and Forum

The Basilica was the commercial and administrative heart of Corinium Dobunnorum *(Cirencester)*, and was where deals were made and laws practised.

The Romans had a highly sophisticated legal system which underpins civil law practised in modern times.

Large statues would have dominated the *Forum (public square)* where the population of the local area could meet. One of these would have been on a 13 metre *(42 feet)* high column. Surrounding the forum were various offices for local administrators and merchants. There would probably also have been market stalls selling food and household items sourced from all over the Roman Empire. Some of the merchants who traded here became very rich and built large villas in the surrounding countryside.

Find out more

There are no visible remains of the Basilica and Forum, shown with the red outlines on the map, except for part of a column found in 1808. Part of the column can be seen in the Corinium Museum. Archaeologists have found evidence of a possible Public Bathhouse located next to the Basilica.

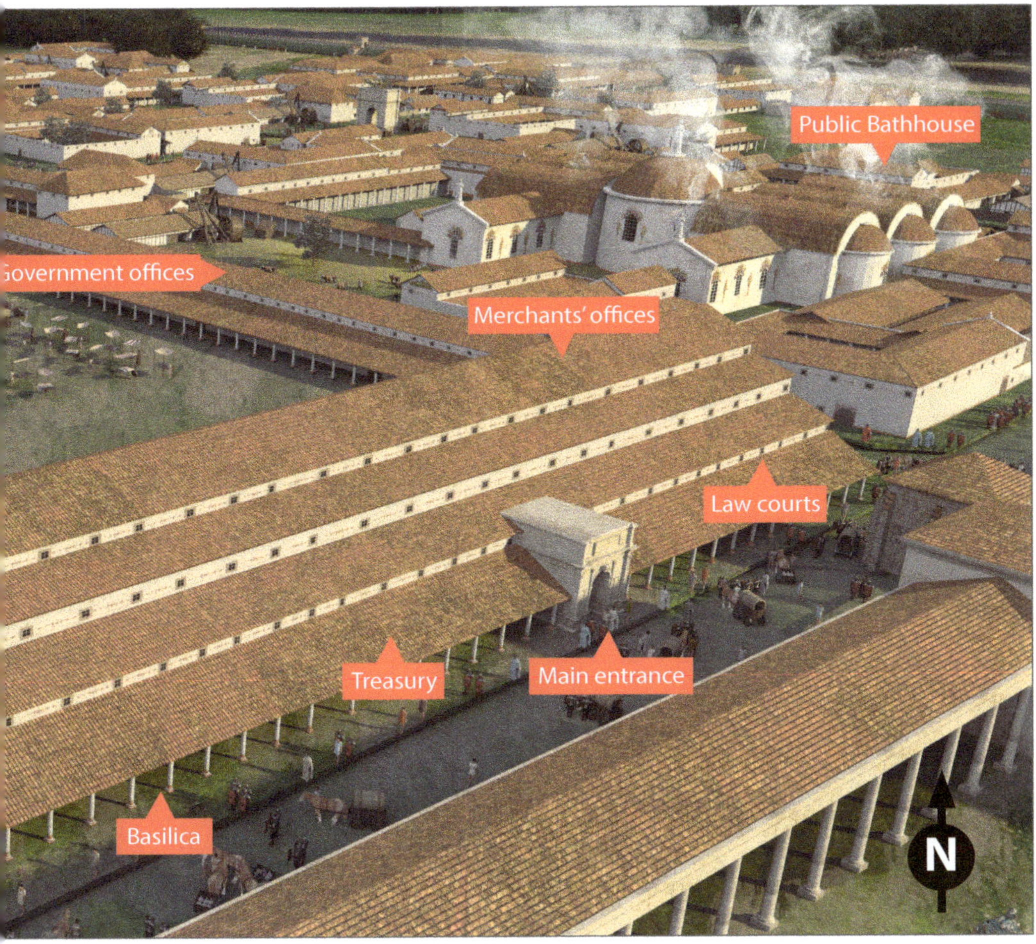

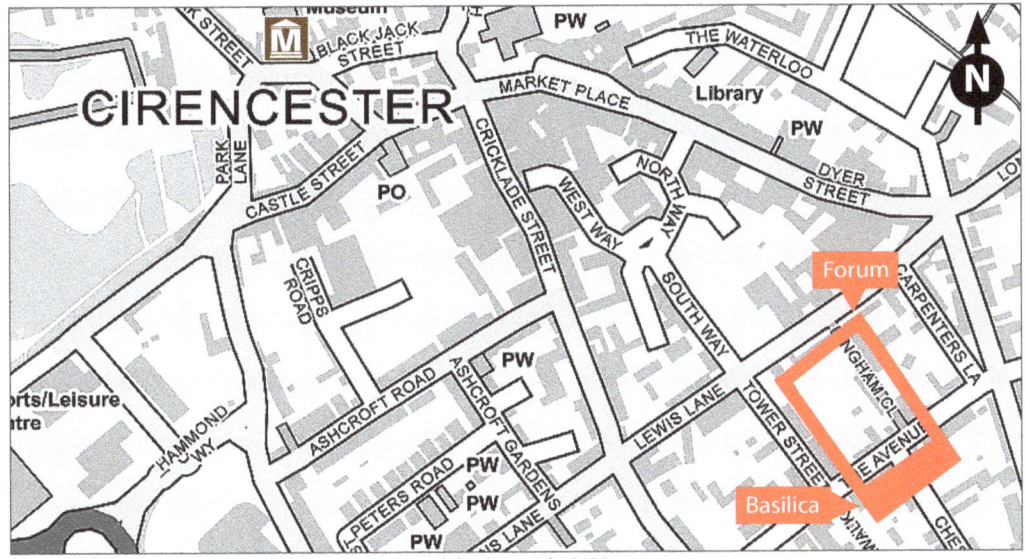

28. The Macellum (Market)

Site of the Macellum (Market), looking north, 200 CE.

The Macellum *(Market)*

Next to the Forum is believed to be the site of a Macellum *(Market)*. A town of this size would have had a large provision market. It is possible that this was a meat market selling meat such as beef and pork. Meat was expensive and was accompanied by cheaper vegetables and fruit, many of which were introduced by the Romans. Cereal crops such as wheat were already cultivated by the native Britons long before the Roman invasion. The Romans had a more varied diet and brought many new plants to cultivate in Britain, such as apples, grapes and many herbs.

They imported foods from across the Roman Empire too, such as olives *(which could not be grown in Britain)* and a popular fish sauce called *garum*. The Romans also had the equivalent of fast food outlets and bakeries which allowed the less wealthy access to cooked food.

Find out more
There are no visible remains of the Macellum, shown on the map with red outlines.

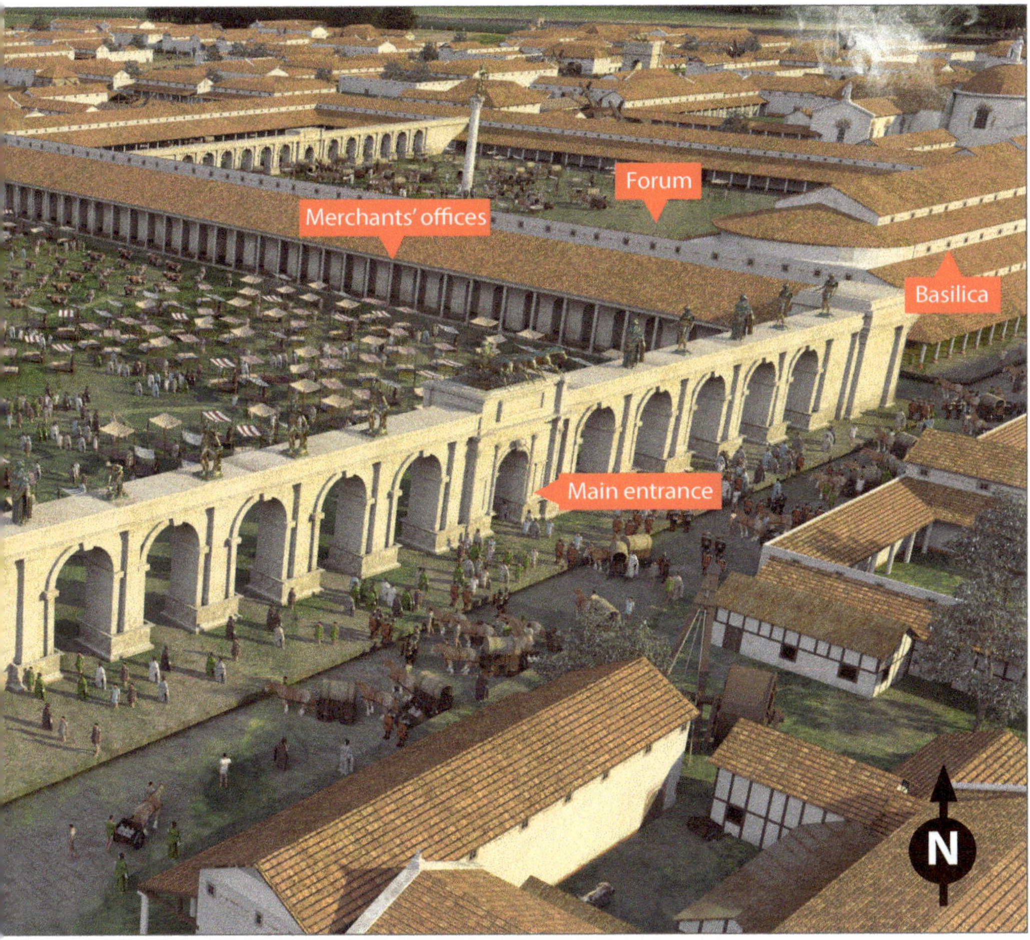

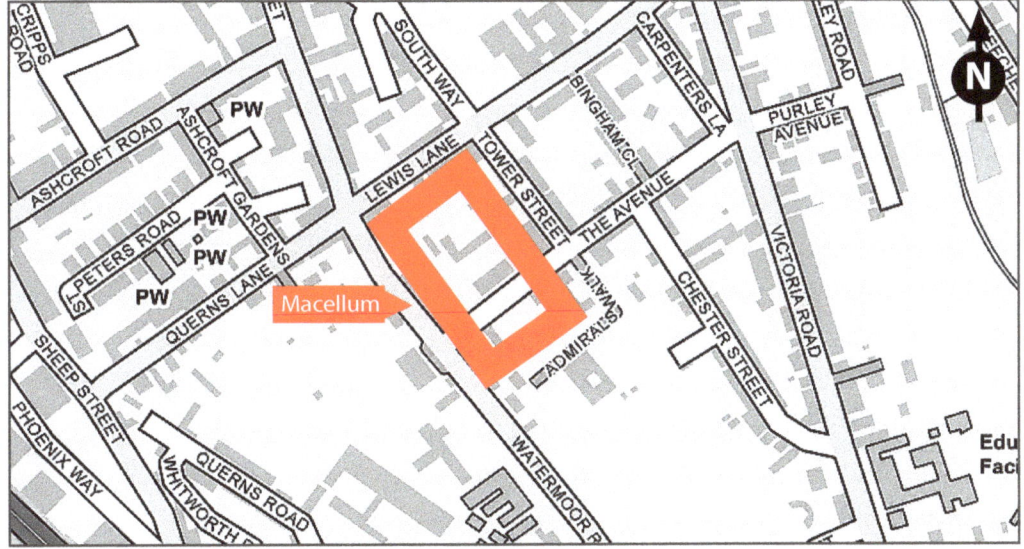

Possible site of the Roman Theatre, looking north, 200 CE.

The Roman Theatre

Archaeologists have found what they believe to be a Roman theatre in the north of the town centre.

Pantomimes were more popular than plays, as well as comedies based on people's lives.

The audience would have entered the theatre through the *Vomitorium* and sat in the semi-circular *Auditorium*, overlooking the *Orchestra (stage)*.

The building may have stood over 20 metres *(60 feet)* tall with a large and complex stage area including the *Scaenae frons*, which was full of columns and provided a background for the actors. Often the actors wore strange masks which represented their characters. Unlike present day actors, Roman actors were not well respected and were often slaves. The seating was strictly controlled with the rich and powerful having the best seats in the theatre.

Find out more

There are no visible remains of the theatre, shown in red on the map.

Note the Triumphal Arch is speculative, although many towns in Roman Britain had them such as at St. Albans, which had two.

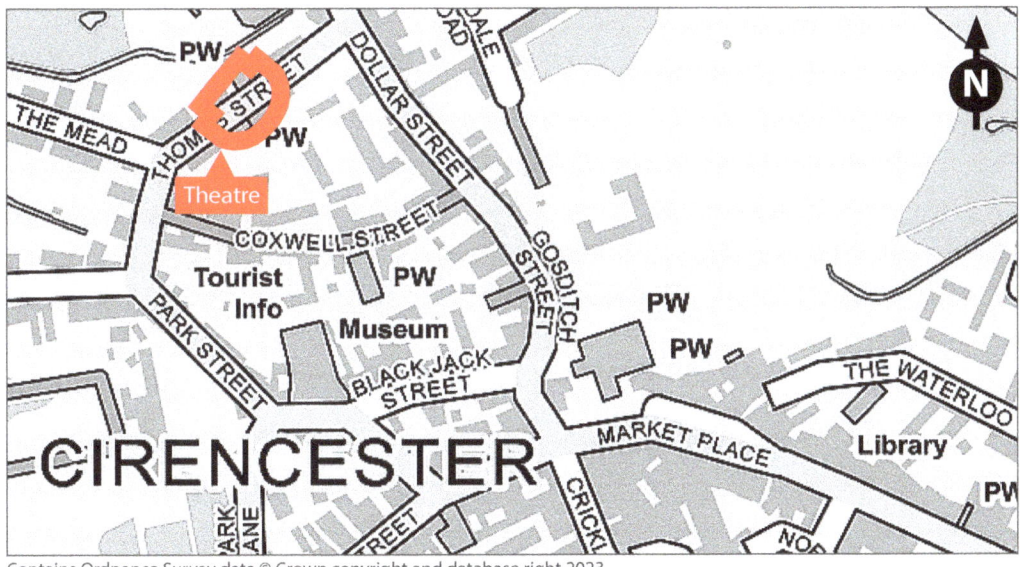

A view showing typical weapons and equipment used by the Second Legion.

The Roman Army

During the initial Roman invasion, the Roman forces were made up of four legions: *Legio II Augusta* (2nd Legion 'Augustus'), *IX Hispana* (9th Spanish Legion), *XIV Gemina* (14th Legion "The Twinned Fourteenth Legion") and *XX Valeria Victrix* (20th Victorious Valeria Legion). The *Legio II Augusta* moved around the south west of Britain, establishing a small fortress in the Cirencester area, possibly manned by a cavalry unit. By the 4th century Roman Britain had been split up into four provinces, with Corinium *(Cirencester)* ruling *Britannia Prima*[1]. Corinium became a major distributor and manufacturer of equipment for the Roman Army. Only in London has more 4th century Roman Army equipment been found, and it is thought that Corinium had a permanent military force.

1. Britannia Prima roughly covered south-west England and Wales.

Find out more
The Corinium Museum has many artefacts from the Roman Army. They include weapons, armour and horse equipment, mostly from the later part of the Roman occupation.

Galea (Helmet)
Lorica Segmentata (Body armour)
Tunica (Tunic)
Caligae (Heavy-duty sandals)

N
BARTON LANE
Education Facility
PW
THE MEAD
THOMAS STREET
DOLLAR STREET
DUGDALE ROAD
SPITALGATE
HEREWARD ROAD
BLAKE
COXWELL STREET
Tourist Info
Museum
BLACK JACK STREET
CECILY HILL
PARK STREET
GOSDITCH STREET
CIRENCESTER
MARKET PLACE
THE WATERLOO
Library
DYER STREET
PARK LANE
CASTLE STREET
PO
CRICKLADE STREET
WEST WAY
NORTH WAY
SOUTH WAY
CRIPPS ROAD
CARPENTERS LA
LONDON R
CORINIUM GA
A 435
The Lake
Sports/Leisure

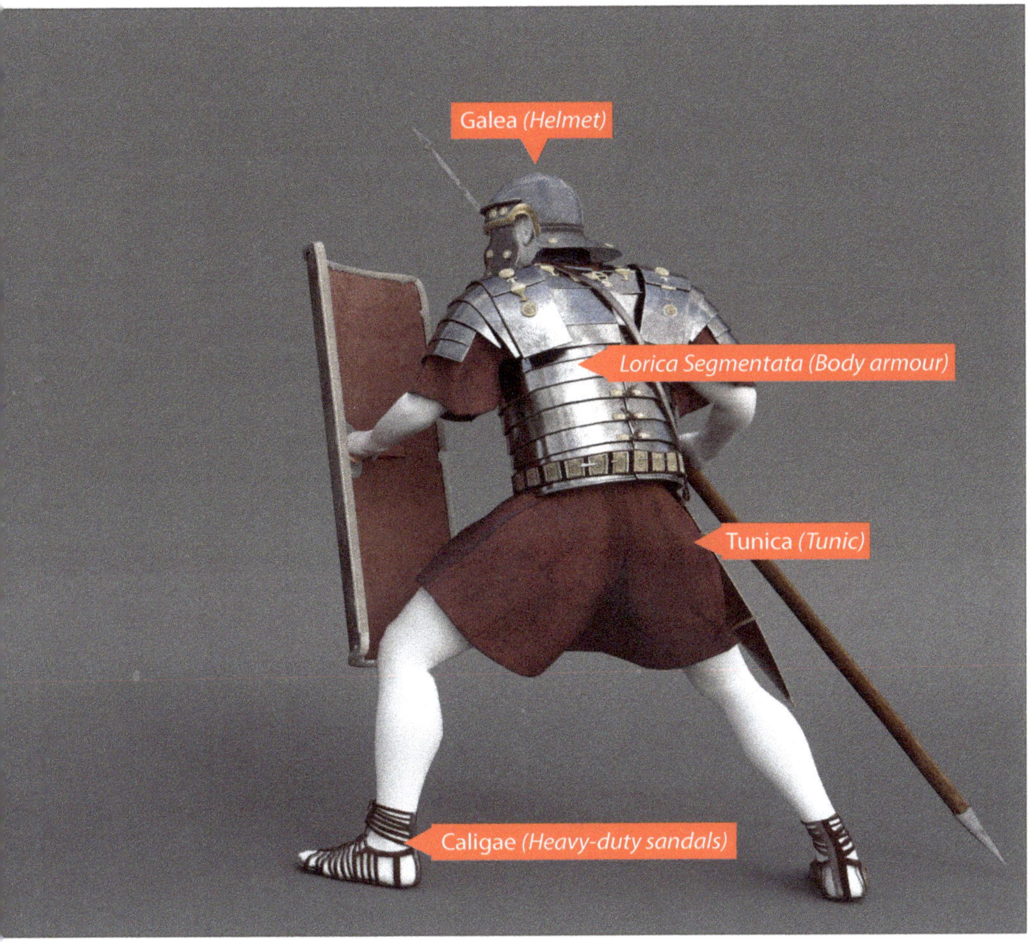

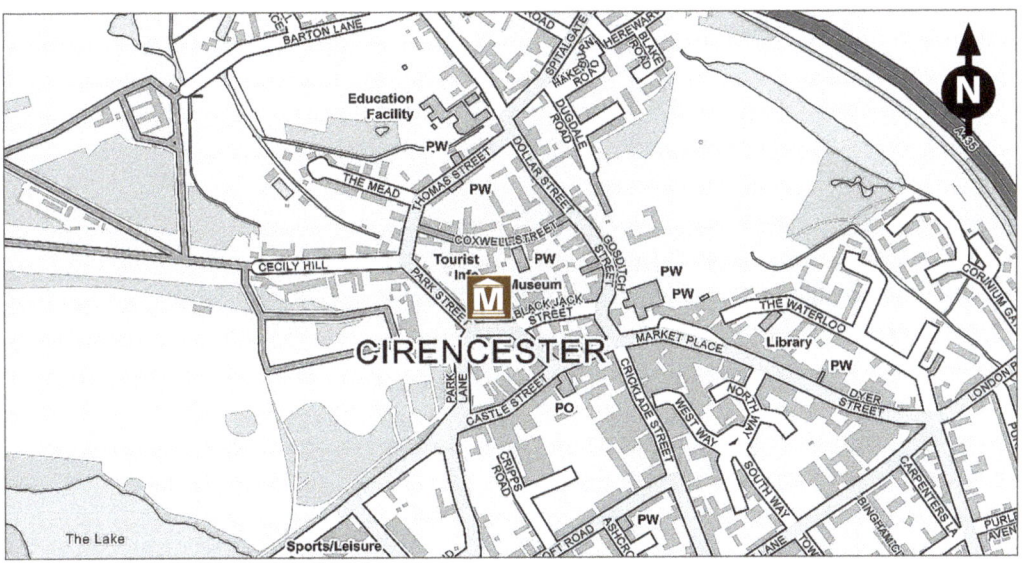

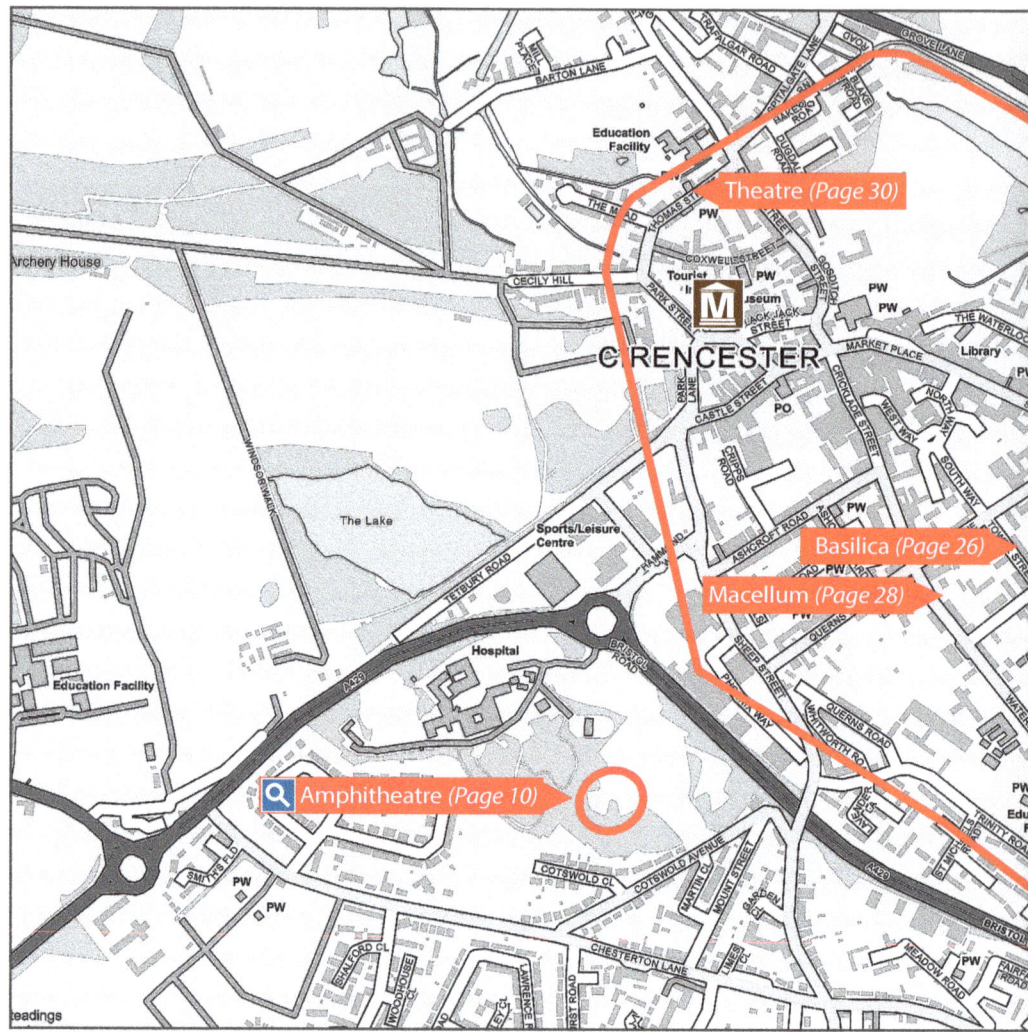

Roman Cirencester today

On this present day map you can see where all the Roman sites mentioned in this book are located.

During the Roman occupation Cirencester became one of Britain's wealthiest towns and its inhabitants owned many beautiful artefacts, including superb mosaics. The Corinium Museum has arguably the best collection of Roman mosaics in the country, as well as excellent exhibits showing life in Roman Cirencester. Many of these are shown throughout this book as they could have looked in Roman times.

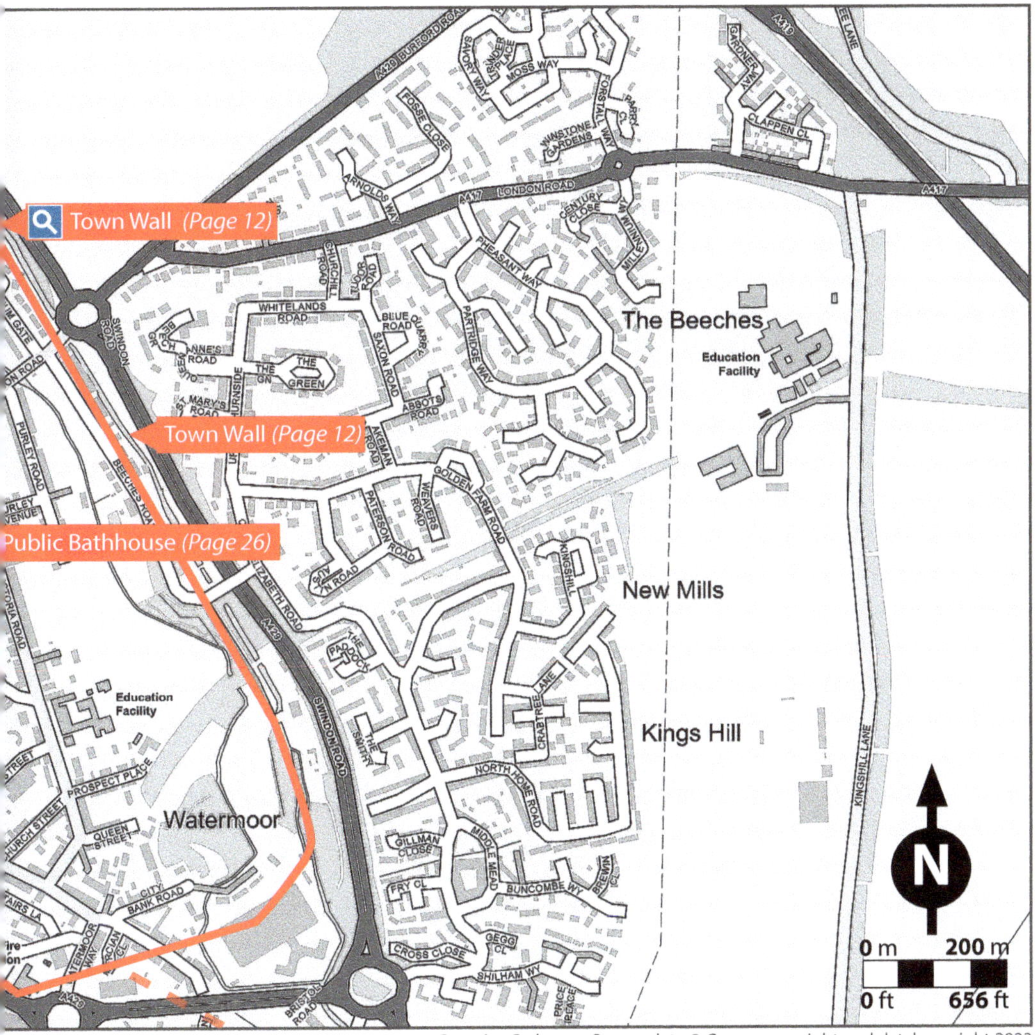

Symbols used on this map

Outlines of Roman walls *(still visible)*

⸻

Outlines of Roman walls *(no longer visible)*

🔍 Amphitheatre *(Page 10)*
Roman points of interest *(still visible)*

Basilica *(Page 26)*
Roman points of interest *(no longer visible)*

 Corinium Museum
Displaying multiple artefacts including:
Hare Mosaic (P 14)
Seasons Mosaic (P 16)
Hunting Dogs Mosaic (P 18)
Orpheus Mosaic (P 20)
The Venus Mosaic (P 22)
Hypocaust (P 24)
The Roman Army (P32)

First published February 2023
ISBN 978-1-7391254-1-7 *(Paperback)*
Second Edition

Designed and published by JC3DVIS
www.jc3dvis.co.uk
Book design © 2023 Joseph Chittenden

All the images in this guide were produced by JC3DVIS.
Contains Ordnance Survey data © Crown copyright and database right 2023

The moral right of the copyright holder has been asserted.

All rights reserved. No part of this publication may be reproduced, distributed or transmitted in any form or by any means, including photocopying, recording, or other electronic or mechanical methods, without the prior written permission of the publisher.

With special thanks to:
Emma Stuart, Corinium Museum
Jane Chittenden
Valerie Graves

Legal disclaimer
Neither the author nor the publisher shall be held liable or responsible to any person or entity with respect to any loss or incidental or consequential damages caused, or alleged to have been caused, directly or indirectly, by the information contained herein.

www.ingramcontent.com/pod-product-compliance
Lightning Source LLC
Chambersburg PA
CBHW040242130526
44590CB00049B/4225